LISTENING TO THE SPIRIT

LISTENING TO THE SPIRIT

Preparation for Confirmation

Group Leader's Book

Carolyn Noar

Collins Dove

Published by COLLINS DOVE
60–64 Railway Road, Blackburn, Victoria 3130
Telephone (03) 877 1333

Illustrated by Nell Frysteen
Designed by Mary Goodburn
Typeset in Times by Solo Typesetting, S.A.
Printed by Impact Printing, Vic.

Listening to the Spirit is part of the Sacramental
Programme from Collins Dove. The planning
committee were Mary-Anne Caleo, Margaret Carman,
Helen Carboon, Margaret Counihan, Philippa Lovell,
Carolyn Noar and Peter Vyverberg.

The Children's Book and Leader's Guide for *Listening
to the Spirit* were prepared by Helen Carboon and
Peter Vyverberg.

Photo Credits: Michael Coyne (pp. 30–31, 42–43,
52–53); Howard Birnstihl (pp. 46–47); David Lovell
(pp. 24–25).

National Library of Australia
Cataloguing-in-Publication data:

Noar, Carolyn.
    Listening to the Spirit, preparation for Confirmation.
    Group leader's book.

    ISBN 0 85924 644 2.

    1. Confirmation—Study and teaching. I. Title.
    (Series: Sacramental Programme).

265′.2′07

Introduction

*S*ince parents have conferred life on their children, they have a most solemn obligation to educate their offspring. Hence parents must be acknowledged as the first and foremost educators of their children.'
And
'While belonging to the family, the task of imparting education requires the help of society as a whole.'

Vatican II Constitution on Education

*F*or eight years I was involved in the development of the Family Sacramental Programme at Holy Spirit Parish, North Ringwood, Victoria.

North Ringwood is a very young parish, established in 1972 to service newly opened housing estates. As there was no parish school at that stage, parents (through necessity) became the religious educators of their children. This role included the important task of Sacramental preparation for the child's first Reconciliation, Eucharist and Confirmation.

At first, children prepared for the Sacraments individually with their families. Some parents felt competent to undertake the preparation task, others wanted help from the parish. This led to the formation of a team of catechists who, with the active support of the parish priest, promoted the importance of family-centred religious education.

As the number of parishioners increased it became necessary to structure the programme. Catechists organised preparation classes in the parish centre to support parents. However, these classes were large and could become impersonal.

Finally, through consultation within the parish between catechists, parish school, parish priest and parents the current model was developed, in which groups of parents and children work together as they prepare for each Sacrament.

The parish invites families to join the programme, offers introductory information at parish meetings for all participants, and organises family groups for home meetings. The parish supports these groups through selecting and training two parent leaders from each group who co-ordinate meetings. They are the vital link between parish organisation and family groups.

As the time for children to receive the Sacrament approaches, all participants meet with the priest for discussion on the significance of the Sacrament, and with catechists to organise the liturgy.

There are four partners in the programme—the family, the church, the catechists and the school. As the people interact, children and adults, faith education happens.

This approach to learning and meeting in neighbouring family groups is modelled on the Family Cluster developed by Dr Margaret Sawin, who believes that families are simultaneously the most valuable and the most threatened structure in the developed world. The more impersonal and confusing the world becomes, the more desperately its members need a family for intimacy, love and acceptance. The model aims to help families develop a deeper knowledge of the Sacraments and stronger bonding through communal celebration.

My family participated in the programme during the years the children attended government schools. The growth and spiritual enrichment we experienced plus the comments of so many participating families convinced me to form a Family Sacramental Programme using Holy Spirit Parish as a model. The programme is challenging and demanding and also full of surprises.

I believe that Family Sacramental Programmes can play a vital role in creating a caring community. This is one model and it can also be adapted for classroom use. Parishes may use it as a guide and reference point from which they develop a programme to suit their needs.

Carolyn Noar

Commonsense wisdom tells us that the family is an extremely important agency for the moral development of children. This wisdom arises from our own experience that our own deepest values and those of people we have observed were formed in the earliest years in the family.

John L. Eliss 'Family Ministry', Winston Press.

Family Catechesis brings the faith back to where it belongs in the first place: to the family. It gives parents back the faith and the responsibility of living out their faith in their own family circle, at their own level.

Wim Saris S.D.B. 'Towards a Living Church', Collins Liturgical.

Communication is at the top of the family specialists' list because it is basic to loving relationships. It's the energy that fuels caring, giving, sharing and affirming. Without genuine listening and sharing of ourselves, we can't know one another.

Dolores Curran 'Traits of a Healthy Family', Winston Press.

The Pope has said that 'the family has the mission to guard, reveal and communicate love' (Familiaris Consortio 17). Through the love of parents for one another and for them, children get the first inkling of God's love for them. Children see God reflected in their parents. The Pope says that the family is called together by word and Sacrament to be the Church, the home is both teacher and mother.

Francis Rush, Archbishop of Brisbane. 'How to Hand on Faith to Your Children', Dove Communications, 1984.

C O N T E N T S

Section I

8

Organising the programme in the parish

Designed for parish organisers this section sets out step by step organisation at parish level.

Preparing the parish for the programme.
Sample letters and notices for parents, parish and schools.
Preparation for talks for parents.
Formation of family groups.
Training and support for group leaders.
Sample programme outline.
Conclusion.

Section II

17

Preparation for Confirmation

Designed for the group leaders, this section gives step by step instructions for coordinating family home meetings.

A family programme
Before the meetings
Introducing the programme
Meeting 1   Remembering.   26
Meeting 2   My Confirmation.   34
Meeting 3   The Holy Spirit.   44
Meeting 4   The Holy Spirit in my life.   48
Meeting 5   Belonging to the Church Community.   56
Meeting 6   Preparation for the Sacrament.   62

Section I

1 Preparing the Parish for the Family Sacramental Programme

Organising the programme in the parish

Designed for parish organisers this section sets out step by step organisation at parish level.

*T*he Church acknowledges that parents are the primary faith educators of their children. However local custom has often delegated this role to the school and the parish. Therefore it is vital for the priest to talk about the important role of parents in the faith education of their children. The homilies at parish Masses offer an opportunity for this. Four to six months before the programme begins is an appropriate time.

During these homilies, the priest would:

- introduce the Family Sacramental Programme to the parish and outline the concept that parents prepare their children for the Sacraments in family groups, supported by teachers and catechists;
- let people know that talks will be given to the parents on the Sacraments to help them to have a better understanding of the Church today;
- introduce the idea that the decision to be confirmed should be made within the family through discussion between parents and students.

During the preparation, the parish and parish council will need to be made aware of the importance of praying for and supporting the families during their year of preparation.

2 Sample letters and notices for parents, parish and schools

*T*he decision to prepare children for the Sacraments calls for a serious commitment. For many parents it may be the first time they have assessed their own attitudes to their faith since their child's Baptism.

It is therefore important to make contact with parents some months before the programme begins.

The sample letter and notice on the two following pages may be photocopied.

Letter to parents

This letter would be given to the parents of children in Years 3, 4, 5 and 6 in the Government schools and the Catholic parish school. It is suggested that this letter be given out by the teachers and catechists in November in preparation for the Sacramental Programme for the following year.

Letter to parents through the parish newsletter

The letter on page 10 should be placed in the parish school newsletter in November of the year preceding the programme, and again in late January and early February of the following year. Where possible, it should also be placed in local government school newsletters. The letter outlines the time schedule for four introductory meetings on the Sacraments.

> My daughter wanted to make her First Communion because of the catechists taking classes at school. She insisted for several years, and I thought if it was her decision she would have a very strong faith. I'm not a practising Catholic and I'm separated from my husband. I've been hurt in the past and have felt bitter. In the small groups I could listen and was amazed at the changes that have taken place within the Church. For me it has been like a 'thawing out'—a beginning.
>
> *Catherine*

Dear Friends,

I am writing to invite you to be part of our Sacramental Programme next year. As you may know, children generally make their First Reconciliation and First Communion in Year 3, and their Confirmation in Year 5 or 6, but of course this may vary, as some parents may prefer to wait until their children are a little older.

In our parish we plan to have four evenings for parents of the children and invite speakers to talk about Baptism and the Church, Reconciliation, Eucharist and Confirmation. These talks and discussions will be low key, informative, and will create an opportunity amongst the people who are there to discuss the changes that have taken place in the Church, and generally bring us up to date with the Sacraments as they are now.

If you have been hurt in the past, or have not been to Church for years, I really ask you to take this opportunity to come back, because we very much want you to be part of our Catholic parish community.

Parents will prepare their children for the Sacraments in small family groups, with the help of teachers and catechists. There will be help available with books, videos and discussion groups. This will be a wonderful opportunity for many adults and children in neighbouring streets to meet and support one another.

The talks, for parents only, will be:

Dates	Time	Place

It is essential that you attend if your child is to receive the Sacraments next year, as the planning and information for the year's programme will be discussed and formed from these nights.

Don't be shy about coming — we will meet you and make you feel most welcome!

Kind regards,
Signed: (Parish Priest)

Preparation for Confirmation
A special message for parents

Dear parents,

Have you a child aged eleven to fourteen years who wishes to receive the Sacrament of Confirmation? This Sacrament marks an important step in your child's response to God.

Please discuss with your child whether this would be the best time to prepare for the Sacrament. If you are unsure, our first four meetings may help you decide.

The parish will begin its programme of Sacramental preparation with four meetings. These will include talks and discussions on the Sacraments and on the Church. We will also outline in detail the development, structure and plan for the Sacramental programme so it is essential that all parents whose children wish to receive these Scaraments attend.

Dates   Time   Place

Our Sacramental programme is family based. The Parish Council invites you to stay for supper and meet other parents who will be involved with you in family groups for Sacramental preparation.

Signed:

3 Preparation for the talks for the parents

*W*hen planning the introductory parents' meetings, it may be helpful to invite speakers from outside the parish who have a special interest in Sacramental preparation or family catechesis. The local Catholic Education Office or Catechetics Centre may help.

When briefing speakers explain the purpose of the talk and describe the audience. If possible meet speakers before the meeting to tell them the story of your parish and its people.

These suggestions may help meetings to progress smoothly:

- the talks are most effective when they are low key, and allow ample time for small group discussion and questions on faith;
- it is important to be aware of the many stages of faith development of the people present;
- the parish council, teachers and catechists play a vital role in welcoming people, and making them feel at home;
- large name tags (large enough to be seen!) need to be available with sufficient pens;
- have ready several large sheets of paper and pens for parents to print their child's name, address, phone number and school;
- since this will be the original record of the people attending these evenings it is important that names and necessary information all be printed clearly;
- a selection of books on the Sacraments, Mass, prayer, saints, children's religious stories and suitable tapes could be made available for purchase at these meetings;
- the priest welcomes the parents and introduces the guest speaker;
- at the conclusion of each talk the priest reminds the parents of the talks in the following weeks;
- the priest asks the parents of children preparing for Reconciliation, First Communion or Confirmation to stay for an extra hour after the talk on the Eucharist for the explanation and planning of the Programme;
- the parish council invite the parents to stay for a cup of tea or coffee and a chat after the talks;

After the third meeting parents should break into the family groups and the group leaders then coordinate an informal discussion on meeting times and venues. Invite families to share their homes for the meetings. Make sure everyone receives a list of the names, addresses and telephone numbers.

4   Formation of the groups

*I*t is suggested that the composition of the groups be decided by the priest, a teacher and a catechist, or by key people involved with the Programme.

- Discernment in forming the groups is important. Ideally:
  - groups should be formed from neighbouring streets;
  - there should be eight to ten children per group (plus parents);
  - each person within the group will be at different stages of faith development;
  - committed Catholics will be mixed with the unchurched;
  - single parents will be mixed with supportive families;
  - ethnic groups will be mixed;
  - both boys and girls will be included in the groups;
  - government school children will mix with parish school children;
  - two leaders should be appointed from within the group, by those responsible at parish level for the formation of the groups.
- Group lists containing names, addresses, phone numbers and the identity of the two leaders for each group are prepared in time for distribution to parents of the First Communion and Reconciliation children at the conclusion of the evening of the third talk.
- At the fourth talk provide each group with meeting times and venues. Group leaders should contact all families before the first home meeting. See page 22.
- It is suggested that home meetings are best kept short, no more than one hour, with a short play time following the meeting.
- The Reconciliation, Eucharist or Confirmation Books should be given to each child in the group before the first family group meeting (see Section 5).

It was good! I got to know other kids from the different schools. When I went to get my medal and certificate after I had made my First Communion, I felt nervous because everyone clapped. Looking back on my First Communion it was friendly and good. It was a nice feeling! Now when I go to Communion, I don't feel so nervous. To know a lot about Communion, I would have to look at my book to remind me.

Belinda

5 Training and support for the leaders of the groups

*T*hose parents invited to be leaders should be contacted before the group lists are presented to the parents on the final night of the talks.

- Further education on sacramental theology will need to be offered to the leaders of the groups, as well as suggestions on group leadership.
- The leaders' evenings should be held over three nights following the talks for the parents.
- Priests, religious or lay people with an understanding of the Programme would be best suited to lead these evenings.
- During the leaders' evenings:
  - There should be ample time for the leaders' own faith questions to be raised.
  - Ideas should be presented to create a welcoming atmosphere at the family group meetings.
  - The leaders should be encouraged to share their own ideas and thoughts for creative activities within the group.
  - Assistance should be given to leaders on how to use the Group Leader's Books with the family groups.
- The Reconciliation, Eucharist and Confirmation Books for the children should be given to the leaders for distribution to each child in the group, with a simple explanation and a request that the child and parents prepare the first section together, before the first family group meeting.

I have been involved with three First Communion Programmes and two Confirmations as a joint leader in each of them. Even though it's the same type of Programme each year, the people are different, therefore each group is new and different. It's better to change the leaders, and allow different people the opportunity to lead and bring in new ideas. Even though my husband wasn't involved with the groups, he would wander in and out of the room when we had the meetings at home, and hear myself and the kids talking about it during the week. Had the kids been going to classes in the parish they would have gone on their own, come home, and that would have been the end of it! The kids met and made new friends, and there was a bonding with the adults. We learnt a lot about our children in the groups, reacting with the other children. We learnt from other parents, listening to the way they talked and explained things to their children. At first it was a bit frightening, and uncomfortable for the parents, but as they went through the Programme they became more confident. My children went to state primary schools, and by being involved with the group we all had the opportunity to get to know each other irrespective of where our children went to school. I have since become more involved in the Parish with parents from the parish school.

Margaret

6 Sample Programme Outline

*S*ince the Family Sacramental Programme must fit in with the Church seasons, parish liturgies and school holidays, it should be planned towards the end of the year *before* the start of the Programme.

- A copy of the Programme dates, together with the lists of the family groups, should be given to the parents after the talks on Reconciliation, Eucharist and Confirmation.

- A careful explanation of the Programme should be given by the priest.

- It is important that parents know the extent of Sacramental preparation offered by teachers or catechists. Representatives of the parish school and the catechists should be available to answer parents' questions at parish meetings.

- The Reconciliation, Eucharist and Confirmation Books should be on display for the parents, with an explanation that these books would be distributed by the group leaders before the first family group meeting.

- The leaders of the groups should be responsible for collecting the money for the books at their meetings.

- It would be helpful to explain to parents that for parish planning purposes, all dates need to be set well in advance.

- On completion of the home meetings the priest may wish to meet with children and parents. Build these meetings into the Programme timetable.

Confirmation meeting with the priest

- Two or three groups could combine to meet with the priest in the parish house before Confirmation.
- The priest should talk about Confirmation and the preparation that has taken place in the family groups with the children and parents. The priest should go through the ritual for Confirmation.
- The preparation for the liturgy for Confirmation should have been done by the priest, teachers and catechists, and should allow as much parental and child involvement as possible.
- At this meeting parents and children should be invited to participate in the Confirmation liturgy.
- A copy of the prepared liturgy should be given to those taking part.

Conclusion

'**P**arents who hand over the [faith] education of their children to others are missing the chance of a lifetime to remain young and grow up with them.'

Wim Saris S. D. B. 'Towards a Living Church' page 11 © South African Catholic Bishops Conference, 1980.

With a Family Sacramental Programme, parents do have the opportunity of growing and learning with their children, and faith education occurs where it belongs—within the family. The Family Sacramental Programme allows:
- an opportunity for parents to re-discover their faith and the Sacraments;
- parents to be better equipped to share and talk about their faith with their children;
- future leaders for the parish to emerge from the parents;
- parents and children to have the opportunity of meeting and getting to know one another through the family groups;
- parents and children to have the opportunity to plan and participate in liturgies;
- a bonding to form within and between families;
- a closer relationship between priest, parents and children to form through more personal contact;
- families to form a real sense of belonging to the parish community.

As I wrote this programme I was walking on a faith journey with so many families with whom I was involved during my years at Holy Spirit Parish. The challenges and demands that were met, the growth and bonding that took place in and between families has convinced me, even more, of the importance of a Family Sacramental Programme. I believe it would contribute to creating a caring community.

We were happy to be involved, but it was tiring and demanding. It was a growing experience for parents and there was a real bonding through the Programme. The children were proud to have their parents involved. Regardless of where children attend school, it's very important to be together. It would have been easy to leave it to the catechists and teachers in the Catholic school, but looking back, it was a family preparation. The younger children were very much part of it, and have a head start. It was really great—a super programme!

Clare and Kevin

It was great! It brought Sue and I closer together having people home for the meetings. The Programme took me back to the basics. Sue got the feeling of what the Church is about. It worried her, being part of it, and not a Catholic. Sue and I became much closer and it strengthened our relationship, and we became much closer to our daughter. It was terrific and very positive.

Richard

Section II

A Family Programme

Preparation for Confirmation

Designed for the group leaders, this section gives step by step instructions for coordinating family home meetings.

*T*he purpose of this book is to enable children and their parents to prepare and celebrate the sacrament of Confirmation as a family unit in the company of other families.

The meetings have been especially prepared so that the child and the parents come to know and understand each other a little better as they create, tell stories, exchange values, listen, share, dream, sing and pray together. Activities will encourage families to cut, paste, decorate, eat and have fun.

For the children

At meetings the child and the parent will encounter one another in new roles and in relationship with other children and other parents. This is a time to strengthen existing bonds and forge new ones.

For the parents

The parents will come to know and cherish their own child more deeply as they perform together the tasks and rituals suggested in the programme.

Parents can learn to be a responsive audience to their child's developing sense of God and community.

Both parents and children are participants in this preparation for the Sacrament. Each is a co-discoverer and co-explorer in an adventure. May they discover together a more caring world.

For the school

Although the programme places emphasis on children working within family groups, both the Student's Books and the meeting formats in this book can be used effectively in the classroom.

Before the meetings

For the group leaders

Meet together before the programme meetings, and spend some time getting to know one another. For example, learn names, find out about other children in the family, discuss ideas about and experience of Confirmation, the common vision of faith, the strengths of your own family of origin and how these affect your lifestyle, pray together. It is up to you, the leaders, to organise the running of the family meetings. You might like to choose another person or family to help along the way.

During the family meetings

Avoid theological debate, 'We could discuss that later, right now what we need to do is this . . .'

Be honest. If you do not know, say so. The Leader's Book is a guide for the family meetings which can be adapted, using your own ideas and activities.

Helpful Suggestions

- be ready on time;
- finish on time;
- within this constraint timing is flexible;
- care must be taken not to stop a good flow of discussion abruptly;
- it is wise to set time limits, which can always be extended for two or three minutes;
- people come to respect a firmly run schedule and appreciate knowing the time limits for working;
- be clear and precise when giving instructions for games, activities, etc.;
- print clearly on large sheets of paper the words of songs, instructions for name tag games, etc.; pin to curtain or stick to wall.

Creating an atmosphere

- it is important to create atmosphere both at the beginning and the end of the meeting;
- on arrival, welcome parents and children and clearly direct them to the first task;
- have lively music in the background;
- at the closure, allow time for the group to come together and reflect;
- dimmed lighting and candles can help to create a reflective, prayerful atmosphere;
- remember that the closure is the last memory of the evening that the parents and children will take away with them.

Setting up the space

- have the room cleared of valuables to avoid breakages;
- push chairs, coffee tables back to allow space for parents and children to sit on the floor (the best mode for communication among parents and children is to sit on the floor facing the centre);
- have tables (e.g. card tables) as work areas for name tags, etc., separate from the main activity space.

Name tags

- large and colourful;
- different shapes (as suggested in each session);
- parents and children to print names clearly.

A box containing paper, pens, scissors, candles, glue, pins, tape etc., needs to be collected and maintained each week.

Sample outline of the programme for each meeting

(written up on large sheet of paper and displayed each week)

Preparation for Confirmation

	Activities	Time allotted
A	Welcome activity name tags, etc.	5–10 minutes
B	Getting-to-know-you activity song/game	10–15 minutes
C	Agreement	5 minutes
D	Main theme activity	20–25 minutes
E	Conclusion	10–15 minutes
F	Supper	15 minutes

The Agreement

It is crucial that the Sacramental programme be a major focus in each family's life during this time.

An informal agreement is made by the leader and families at the first meeting to focus family commitment. Leave time for discussion of reasons for it. Allow people in the group to express their feelings on the points drawn up if they wish. It is strongly suggested that the original Agreement made at the first meeting be printed clearly on a large sheet of paper and brought to each meeting and pinned to the curtain or stuck to the wall alongside the Outline of Programme.

Suggestions for the Agreement are set out as follows:
1   time and place of the meetings
2   all agree to attend and participate
3   arrive on time
4   contact person for the group (name and phone number)
5   space and rules within the home, boundaries, etc.
6   directions for toilet
7   money matters, including a contribution towards cost of materials to be used at the meetings
8   smoking/non-smoking (boundaries)
9   simple supper arrangements
10 tidy up at conclusion of meeting
11 children complete the following theme in their books and bring to the next meeting.

At each session read the Agreement and amend or delete where necessary. In this way it can reflect the group's work and changes.

The children's opinions need to be encouraged and respected by all.

The Agreement provides a very good model for children to remind them of how differences were resolved.

The Agreement is a way of:
- involving all families;
- developing a working framework that respects all ages and ensures all kinds of people a place in the group;
- setting guidelines and norms for working;
- stating the ways change can take place.

The Agreement can be difficult and may be unpopular at first. But if the groups persevere it will achieve a consensus and cohesion that enables good discussion.

Enjoy your time together, be flexible . . . have fun!

A listening community

Gerard Fourez, S. J., in his book *Sacraments and Passages*, writes about the tensions the community experiences with respect to the newly confirmed.

A community is always slightly anxious in the face of its new members, since they will bring with them a breath of fresh air and new ideas. If they are adult, they will have lived other experiences and traditions. If they are young, they will challenge many routines. That is why the community is often tempted to control them by asking them to involve themselves in accordance with the community's own idea of what they should be.

This is a special temptation for parents; do they not, too often, desire their children to be carbon copies of them? On the other hand, they are easily put off when young people adopt different directions that differ from theirs; in such cases, they feel challenged. Many of them are therefore afraid of this period when their children take their independence.

The Church too sometimes fears new members and especially the young; it then succumbs to the temptation to propose oversimplistic images of what a 'good committed Christian' is, as if it were possible to say in advance where the Spirit will lead people. Hence the ideology of 'commitment' is stressed in connection with Confirmation.

Gerard Fourez, S.J. *Sacraments and Passages*, Ave Maria Press, Indiana 1983 p.88

The community is called to 'listen to' the newly confirmed, who have something original to say: they must be taken seriously. People are 'confirmed' and changed by the fact that the community listens. Without this, it is difficult for them to believe that the Spirit of God is in them.

Introducing the programme

Confirmation

*B*efore beginning the programme it will be necessary for the leaders of each family group to contact the families who will be in the group.

This contact, whether by letter or a home visit, will be an introduction and a welcome to the programme, as well as explaining the time and place and the preparation to be completed in the Student's Book before the first home meeting.

The teachers should be teaching that at school, that's why I pay school fees, was my thought when I first heard that I, as a single mother, would have to carry this responsibility. Religion for me had been mass on Sundays with many distractions with little children, but the four talks on the Sacraments brought me up to date — it was wonderful! I loved the group meetings and it was important to me to have some people in the group I knew already, and were a support for me. The children were very enthusiastic, and had they been taught at school, they would have known more than me. I felt a responsibility in the group, and had to be involved. I thought 'Isn't this wonderful for me!' I learnt with my children.

Catherine

My initial re-action was why should we? ... our children go to a Catholic school. I felt incapable, out of touch, not much growth in faith since primary school, and very apprehensive talking with my child about God. The four talks on the Sacraments were a milestone, and when the Programme finished, I joined a small renewal of faith group. It was a commitment, and nice to be working with my own child. It was an opportunity to introduce prayer. Children take in what you least expect, and see things in different ways. It was full of surprises!

Janet

The programme has meant much to me, because it has fostered real understanding that the parent is the person to whom God entrusted the job of teaching his children about Him. To find a Programme supporting parents and actually challenging them to take on this role regardless of where their children attend school was indeed a rich find. To my husband and I, it meant questioning our own faith development and commitment to ensure we were capable of fulfilling that role. My husband felt he had lacks, so enrolled in adult education programmes in the parish. I needed to know others were in the same boat as we were, struggling with their own faith questions. So it was the support which was vital to me at the time.

Dianne

WELCOME!

Dear

    We are writing to remind you of our meetings for the Confirmation Programme.

    The first meeting will be on ....at................................. at the home of .... Phone...............................

    In preparation for the first meeting could you please read and work through 'Remembering Growing, growing, growing' of the Student's Book? Don't forget to bring the book and some textas along to the meeting.

    We look forward to seeing you all,

Yours sincerely,

Leaders

Remembering

Preparation

- paper (poster size)
- name tags with names on them
- butcher's paper
- some large sheets of paper
- thick textas
- Bible ('Good News' translation is appropriate)
- cassette player
- tape: 'Take it for Gift', Joe Wise
- words of 'Here is my Life' on large sheet

Welcome activity

As each family arrives the leader greets them and hands them their name tags. The leader invites each family to complete the activity on Decision-making in the Student's Book, p. 12.

Game: 'Clumps', a grouping game

1 The leader invites everyone to stand up.
2 Leader: Make fours, Make threes, Make twos and tell each other your name.
3 After a couple of turns at quickly making the clump of the required number, the leader adds an instruction to each number, e.g.
Make twos . . . tell each other your name.
Make fours . . . tell each other your favourite food.
Make fives . . . tell each other a country you would like to visit.

Everyone sits down

*T*he leaders welcome everyone to the programme, and as there will be ongoing meetings, there will be some questions about what is going on.

Agreement

*D*isplay a printed copy of the Agreement (p. 20) and talk about it. Add any other matters.

Keep this section brisk and short. Assure the group that there will always be part of the evening reserved for amendments or deletions.

Looking at the home activity

*T*he leader refers back to the Home Activity completed before this session.
• What was it like to do?
• What did you like about it?
• Who did it with you?
• Any questions? And so on . . .

Home activity for Meeting 2

*R*ead 'History and background of Confirmation' and 'Who should I choose as sponsor?'

Main activity

*T*he leader invites each family to read together 'David', p. 14 of the Student's Book.

Invite students to decide for David. Discuss each decision then continue reading. Invite discussion using the questions in the text.

Then sum up: 'We have been talking about decision-making tonight. We talked about the decisions we make for ourselves, the decisions other people make for us. Now we will look at the decisions Jesus made. Please turn to p. 16 of the Student's Book.'

The leader reads Luke 2:41–50, Student's Book, and adds: 'We now learn about the consequences of Jesus' decision. Complete pp.18–19 of your Student's Book.'

The leader invites some of the students to briefly read the story they have written in their book, about the person who decided to follow Jesus.

Conclusion

*E*veryone gathers in a circle, with the students making the decision about Confirmation, making an inner circle. The leader invites everyone to think of each of the young people by name and to pray for them as we listen to and sing along with 'Here is my Life' by Joe Wise.

Supper

On the way to Emmaus—'Did not our hearts burn within us as he talked to us on the road and explained the scriptures to us.'

Luke 24:32

Here Is My Life

Joe Wise

Refrain

Here is my life, my - self the
bread that I bring.
Here is my soul, my
wine the song that I sing.
Take it for gift and
take it for grant - ed, sprung from the
seeds that I've washed and I've plant - ed

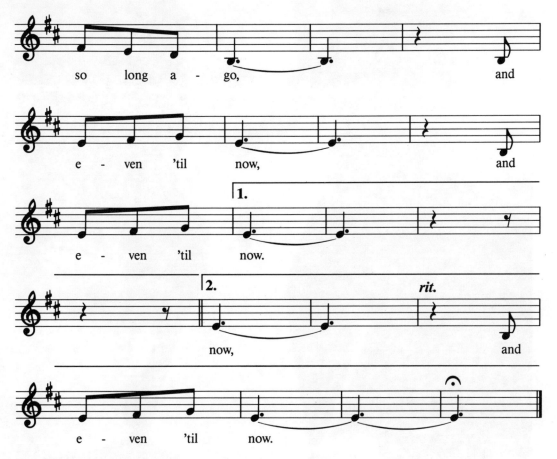

so long a - go, and

e - ven 'til now, and

1. e - ven 'til now.

2. now, *rit.* and

e - ven 'til now.

Here Is My Life

1. Bread from the fields, from my friends
   And bread from the lean years,
   Bread from my youth and my loves
   And bread from the green years.
   This much is ready now,
   This much is ready now,
   This much is ready now.
   Bake it as your own.

2. Wine of my joys and my dreams
   And wine of my good times,
   Wine of my won't and my will,
   My did and my should times.
   This much is ready now,
   This much is ready now,
   This much is ready now.
   Pour it as your own.

3. Bread from the highlands of life
   And bread from the valleys,
   Bread from the good things we've known
   That nobody tallies.
   Now we are ready, Lord,
   Now we are ready, Lord,
   Now we are ready, Lord.
   Bake us as your own.

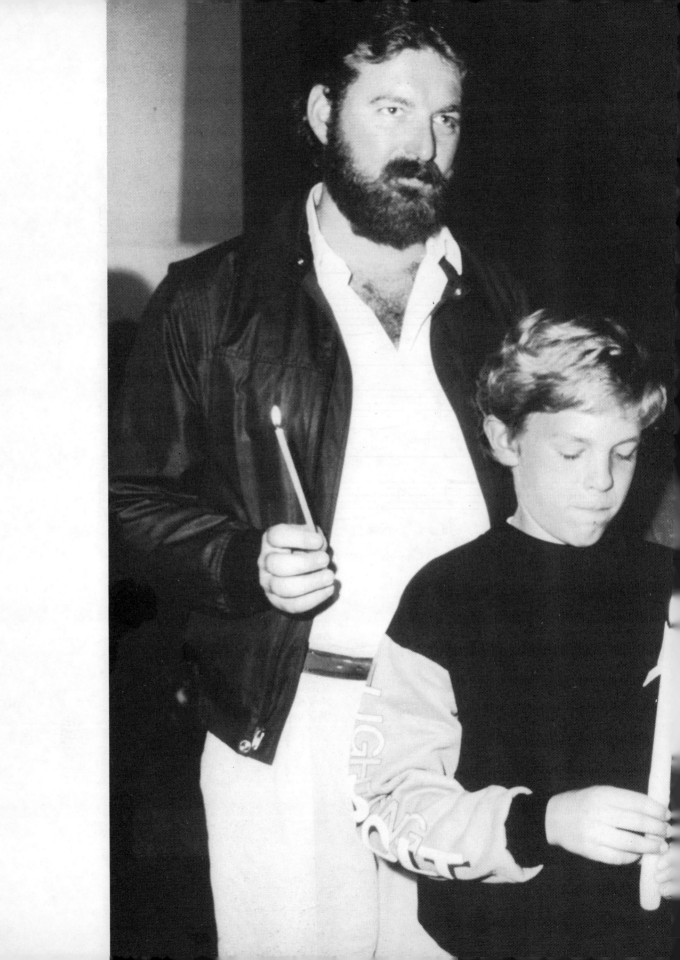

My Confirmation

History and background of Confirmation

To *assist our children adequately in preparing for the Sacrament we need to know something of its history and background. We have used Chapter 61 of J. D. Crichton's comprehensive text 'Christian Celebration' as a basis for the brief summary that follows.*

Confirmation is now recognised as being part of the liturgy of Christian initiation. All the new documents on Christian initiation speak of Baptism, Confirmation and the Eucharist as being the Sacraments by which people are made Christians and assume that this is the order in which they are going to be received. This can come as a surprise, given the present practice for Confirmation to be celebrated after First Communion, usually between the ages of eleven and fourteen. However, the earliest history of the Church shows that from the time Confirmation appeared for the first time as an identifiable rite at the beginning of the third century, Baptism, Confirmation and Eucharist were linked. Even with infants, Confirmation was administered in the early Church immediately after Baptism and followed by the Eucharist.

By the tenth century the ancient order of Christian initiation had largely broken down except in the Eastern Church. Baptism, which was given almost immediately after birth, was no longer celebrated within the Easter vigil. If the bishop was not available, as was often the case, Confirmation was delayed indefinitely. In addition, strong feelings that frequent Communion was inappropriate meant that it was no longer given to infants at Baptism. The age of Confirmation increased during the Middle Ages to twelve or even fourteen.

Crichton believes that in the New Testament all the effects of Baptism and Confirmation are concentrated in Baptism, and Confirmation, as Christians in later centuries have come to know it, is an unfolding in the content and context of Baptism. He says:

Perhaps the failure to realise that the Spirit is active wherever there is faith and Sacrament has created difficulties for an understanding of Confirmation. The Spirit is active in the Holy Eucharist. Too frequently, popular catechesis has given the impression that at Confirmation the Spirit is given for the first time.

J. D. Crichton, *'Christian Celebration'*, Geoffrey Chapman, London, 1971. 1981 edition, p. 101, Chapter 6, author's footnote, 34.

Since the Second Vatican Council, there has been a much greater recognition that parents have a key role in preparing their children for First Communion and Confirmation. As the order of the Sacrament indicates, they do so 'by forming . . . their children . . . in the spirit of faith' and by supporting others who may instruct them. In preparing for Confirmation we must now take account of the fact that the practice of the last one thousand years in which the Sacrament has been a separate rite, differs from the earliest history of the church when even infants were given Baptism, Confirmation and Communion in the same ceremony. The most important consequence of this insight is to realise that the Spirit is present in our earliest Sacramental actions, and that the rite of Confirmation as it will be administered to the children is yet a further unfolding of the presence of the Spirit.

Preparation

- name tags with names written on
- agreement displayed
- pencil
- Confirmation name cards
- filmstrip *Anointed in the Spirit* (Catholic Audio Visual Centre, Homebush, NSW)
- cassette player
- tape 'Lord of Light', St Louis Jesuits

Welcome activity

As each family arrives, invite the students to do the word puzzle from Special Confirmation words in their book (p. 26). Have 'Here I Am Lord' playing on tape.

Game

Isshy game

Leader holds up a pencil giving it the name 'Isshy'. The group sits in a circle, the leader takes the pencil saying,
    'This is Isshy
    My name is . . .

The person I most enjoyed talking to last week about Confirmation
was . . .'
(This sentence may be changed according to the group or the discretion of
the leader.) The pencil is then passed to the next person who says:
'This is Isshy,
That person's name is . . .
My name is . . .
The person I most enjoyed talking to last week about Confirmation
was . . .'
Again the pencil is passed on, and continues until each person in the group
has had a turn.

Agreement

- have the Agreement from last week on display;
- review/amend/delete where necessary.

Looking at the home activity

- The leader talks about the history of Confirmation, drawing from the group their thoughts, insights and queries.

Home activity for Meeting 3

- Do the puzzle 'Be sealed with the Holy Spirit'.
- Read through the first section of Meeting 3 on the Holy Spirit. Read the scripture texts and write a prayer to the Spirit.

Main activity

*H*ave everyone stand and stretch before continuing with main activity.
The leader reads the parts of the ceremony with the group from the
Student's Book, pp. 22–23.

1 The Presentation of candidates: The priest, on behalf of the candidates,
asks the Bishop to accept them for Confirmation into the whole Church.

2   The Homily—the Bishop talks to the candidates: The candidates are welcomed by the Bishop, and encouraged to live out the faith as Confirmed Christians in word and action.

3   Renewal of Baptismal Promises—your commitment to Jesus: The candidates are invited to openly confess their faith before the whole Church and promise to live by it.

4   Laying on of Hands—a special blessing for the candidates: Through the laying on of hands, the Bishop and priests invoke the presence of the Holy Spirit and call on the Spirit to develop and bring to fruition the faith of the candidate.

5   Naming and Anointing—accepting your chosen name: The candidates accept their Confirmation name and are anointed with the oil of chrism. This symbolises their commitment to faith.

6   Sign of Peace—sharing Christ's peace: The Bishop, following the example of Christ, gives the sign of peace and through this sign calls the candidate to go out and share Christ's peace with others.

The role of the sponsor

The leader will continue discussing with the group the role of the sponsor in Confirmation.

Role of the sponsor at the ceremony
- the sponsor sits with the candidate;
- the sponsor proceeds with the candidate to the Bishop;
- the sponsor presents the name card to the priest;
- the sponsor places his or her right hand on the candidate's right shoulder;
- the sponsor and candidate return to their seats.

Following Confirmation
- the sponsor welcomes the candidate to the Church community, and shows example in life and faith by sharing and showing care for the faith life of their candidate.

Choice of sponsor
The choice of a sponsor for Confirmation is very personal and should involve the elements of friendship, closeness, modelling, and a living example of his or her faith life. The following are some examples of possible choices (leaders beforehand may need to check local practices):
a   candidates' godparents: this links the initial Sacrament of Baptism with Confirmation, and re-affirms the role the godparents accepted at Baptism;
b   candidates' parents: as educators in faith parents give the fullest expression to their continuing support for the life of faith in their child;

c   a relative or close friend: this person often is close to the candidate as a model of faith, is closely associated with their everyday life and may be seen to be approachable in times of greatest need.

Eligibility of sponsors

Here the leader needs to be aware of the local requirements as determined by the Bishop. Under the Code of Canon Law (Chapter 4, Canon 872–74) the sponsor must:

i   be suitable for this role and have the intention of fulfilling it;

ii   be not less than 16 years of age, unless a different age has been stipulated by the diocesan Bishop;

iii be a Catholic who has been Confirmed, and has received the blessed Eucharist, and who lives a life of faith which befits the role to be undertaken;

iv   not labour under canonical penalty (be permitted to receive the Sacraments) whether imposed or declared.

Significance of a name

- Keeping Baptism name: this reaffirms the name chosen at Baptism and the significance that Confirmation confirms the faith accepted by others for the candidates at Baptism.
- Choosing another name: in choosing another name we are recognising that the person whose name we choose is a person of faith on whom we would like to model ourselves.

Confirmation name cards

If appropriate, the leader may give out a Confirmation name card to be taken home, filled in, and returned next week.

Conclusion

Prayer reflection

*T*he leader invites the group to stand, join hands and sing together, 'Here I Am Lord' *or* if available, the leader may screen the filmstrip *Anointed in the Spirit.*

Supper

Spirit

A *very difficult Hebrew word to translate is* ruah. *At times it is variously translated by 'breath', 'wind', 'spirit', but it is not exactly any of these. It is the force behind life and behind dynamic activity. Breath is the sign or the principle of life. When people stop breathing, they are dead, in Hebrew thinking. Hence* ruah *can be the breath of Yahweh. This breath of Yahweh is a force that brings about what he wants. It stirred up the Judges to lead the Hebrew people in time of peril; it inspired the prophets to berate the people. In all cases it bestows everything required for the fulfilment of the task at hand. Thus, the Spirit of Yahweh comes to be seen almost as a separate entity, which saved and created and raised people up, just as Yahweh saw fit.*

In the New Testament the word is used with basically the same symbolism. The Spirit is the divine, dynamic force, which now moves the apostles to preach and to witness. It endows them with those capacities required for the task. Particularly in Paul's writings, the Spirit dwells first of all in Jesus himself. At the same time the Spirit pervades the body of Jesus, which is the church. Individual believers also possess the Spirit. Here the symbols of Spirit and Temple combine, for the Spirit is seen as the dynamic forcefulness of God dwelling in the Temple, which is the body-person of the believer. In the individual, the Spirit acts as the principle of life and activity proper to

Christian living: praying, using the various gifts useful in the Christian community, witnessing to Jesus, believing, hoping and, of course, loving:

. . . if you are guided by the Spirit you will be in no danger of yielding to self-indulgence, since self-indulgence is the opposite of the Spirit . . . What the Spirit brings is very different: love, joy, peace, patience, kindness, goodness, trustfulness, gentleness and self-control . . . Since the Spirit is our life, let us be directed by the Spirit. (Galatians 5:16–17a, 22, 25)

There is no explicit identification of the Spirit as a separate divine, personal being in the writings of Paul. That point is almost reached, however, in John. John presents the Spirit as the Paraclete, which means something like 'Helper'. In 1 John 2:1 Jesus himself was identified as a Paraclete, an intercessor before God on behalf of sinners. Jesus promises his disciples, in John's gospel, that he will send another *Paraclete, he being the first. The Second Paraclete will be the Spirit who is identified as the Spirit of Holiness (i.e. of God) or the Spirit of Truth.*

Introduction to the Gospels, Robert Crotty, Shirley Macdonald, Student Book, Collins Dove, 1987.

The Holy Spirit

Preparation

- instructions for welcome activity
- names of the Holy Spirit printed onto cards

  helper   strengthener   leader

  reminder   comforter   supporter

  friend   power
- Bible
- candle, matches

Welcome activity

*H*ave these instructions displayed in a prominent place and direct each family to them as they arrive.

Three of the most often used symbols for the Holy Spirit are:

- wind
- fire
- breath.

Each Scripture quote mentions one of these symbols.

For each of the Scripture quotes on p. 29, choose which symbol is being used. Underline the word(s) which show you this. This activity also looks back on last meeting's home activity.

Game

*T*he leader recalls the names of the Holy Spirit that each family had worked out in the previous week's home activity.

- The leader shows the prepared cards and spreads these on the floor.
- People are then invited to choose their favourite name for the Holy Spirit and stand near it.
- They may then tell the others who also chose their card why this name is their favourite.

Agreement

- Have Agreement on display, adding or deleting information as appropriate.

Home activity

- Give the instructions for next week: read 'The Gifts of the Spirit' and 'The Spirit of Jesus is present'. Read and complete the 'The Spirit of Jesus in my life' pp. 38–41, Student's Book.
- Complete the section on 'peace makers', including writing your story about a peace maker.

Main activity

*I*nvite a young person to read 'What is the Spirit?'

Leader:
a   Just as the Holy Spirit was with the prophets, the Spirit is with Mary and Jesus. We listen to the words of Scripture.
    Reader 1: Luke 1:31–36
    Reader 2: Luke 3:21–22
b   Now, Jesus promises his Spirit to us. In your family group read 'Jesus promised his followers that he would be with them always'. After you have read these quotations, choose your favourite, and use it to write your prayer to the Holy Spirit. Write it on p. 31 of your book and decorate your page.

Conclusion

*G*ather the group around a lighted candle and have each Confirmation candidate pray his or her prayer.

Supper

The Holy Spirit in My Life

Preparation

*A*t this meeting we highlight the gifts and fruits of the Spirit within our lives. The leaders will need to have prepared in advance:

a sign, printed and displayed	Take a gift card for each person who has come with you tonight. Decorate and fill in the card, choosing the gift you would like for that person from the list. Wrap it carefully, label it and put it on the Present Table.
gift cards (on table) textas ribbon sticky tape wrapping paper	Dear . . . . I see the gift of . . . . in you when . . . . Love from . . . .
lists of gifts (printed and displayed)	Happiness Consideration Caring Friendship Strength Helpfulness Kindness Reliability Creativity Fun

sign—'PRESENT TABLE'—to be placed near a small table on which all the 'presents' will be placed.

Prepare a scroll (see p. 42) for each person being confirmed. Name each scroll, role it and place inside the Big Present Box. Display on the present table.

Leaders will also need:
- Bible
- cassette player
- tape 'Come now Holy Spirit' (*Turn it all Around*), Peter Kearney
- words for song printed and displayed

SCROLL INSTRUCTIONS

. . . . (person's name)

I see the gift of . . . .

in you when . . . .

. . . . (Person's name)

I see the gift of . . . .

in you when . . . .

Definitions — See Student's Book p. 42

Wisdom: . . . .

Understanding: . . . .

Right judgement: . . . .

Courage: . . . .

Knowledge: . . . .

Reverence: . . . .

Wonderment and awe in his presence: . . . .

Welcome activity

*A*s each family arrives, direct them to the Gift Card activity. As they complete filling out their gift card and wrapping it as a present, show them where to put it on the 'Present Table'. The gift giving will remind the group of their home preparation reading on the gifts of the Spirit.

Song

*S*itting on the floor, sing together: 'Come now Holy Spirit'.

Agreement

*H*ave Agreement displayed. Amend/Delete, where necessary.

Home activity

*R*ead and complete activities on pp. 43–49 in the Student's Book. Make a 'Sacramental Stole', p. 50.
- Each family should bring a Bible to the next meeting.
- Bring Baptism 'souvenirs' for next week's meeting, e.g., stoles, candles, photos, etc.

Main activity

*T*he leader takes the 'big present' from the present table and places it in the centre of the room. Stimulate the group's curiosity:
- What do you think is in it?
- What would you like?
- Is it heavy or light?
- Who'd like to open it? And so on . . .

Choose someone to open it and distribute a scroll to each person to be confirmed. The parents and children read the definition of each gift on p. 42 of the Student's Book. Then they choose the particular gift that they see most often in each other and complete the gift section on the scroll.

Conclusion

A prayer about gifts

Leader: If everyone in the world used the natural gifts given by the Holy Spirit and appreciated by everybody, what a beautiful place it would be! It is the Spirit of God who has the power to make our world new.

Give and unwrap gifts from the Welcome activity.

Reader: Revelations 21:3–5

Sing again: 'Come now Holy Spirit'.

Supper

Come Now Holy Spirit
(Veni Sancte Spiritus)

Peter Kearney

Come now Ho - ly Spi - rit, come now, Strong like wind and bright like fi - re; Come through us, oh help and guide us, Bold - ly come and make the Earth all new!

Come to us oh Fa - ther of the poor, Change for joy what we en - dure, Come and bring your peace, your jus-tice and re-lease— Come

break - ing down our door... Spi - rit come!

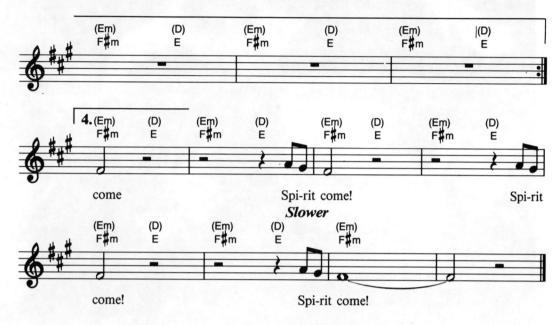

come   Spi-rit come!   Spi-rit

come!   Spi-rit come!

      (Em)   (D)   (Em) (D)
      F♯m   E   F♯m   E
2. Heal our wounds, our strength renew,
      (Em) (D) (Em)   (D)
      F♯m   E   F♯m   E
  On our dryness pour your dew,
      (Bm)   (A)
      C♯m   B
  Wash the stains of guilt away,
      (Bm)   (A)   (Bm)
      C♯m   B   C♯m
  Guide our steps when we would go astray;
      (Em)   (D)   (Bm)
      F♯m   E   C♯m
  Bend our stubborn heart and will, we pray,
      (Em)   (Bm)
      F♯m   C♯m
  Melt the frozen, warm the chill—
      (Em)   (Bm)
      F♯m   C♯m
  Blessed light divine, within our heart come shine,
    (C)   (Em) (B7)   (Em) (D)(Em) etc.
     D   F♯m C♯7   F♯m E F♯m etc.
  Our inmost being fill ... Spirit come!

      (Em) (D)   (Em) (D)
      F♯m E   F♯m E
3. Come today and come tomorrow—
      (Em) (D) (Em) (D)
      F♯m E F♯m   E
  Solace in the midst of sorrow.
      (Bm)   (A)
      C♯m   B
  Pleasant coolness in the heat,
      (Bm)   (A)   (Bm)
      C♯m   B   C♯m
  Welcome rest when labour is complete;
      (Em)   (D)   (Bm)
      F♯m   E   C♯m
  Where you can't be found our lives distort,
      (Em)   (Bm)
      F♯m   C♯m
  Nothing good in deed or thought,
      (Em)   (Bm)
      F♯m   C♯m
  Nothing free from ill, no one can fulfil
    (C)   (Em) (B7)   (Em) (D) (Em) etc.
     D   F♯m   C♯7   F♯m E F♯m etc.
  The need which you have wrought ... Spirit come!

Belonging to a Church Community

Preparation

*T*he leader will need to bring to the meeting:
- posters, books about Christian heroes
- a large ball of wool
- a bowl of water
- a cottonwool ball soaked in oil
- a loaf of bread or Lebanese bread
- a wine glass of grape juice
- a candle

Game

Wool structure

Taking the large ball of wool the leader asks the group to stand in a circle.

The ball of wool is thrown at random across the circle. As people catch it, they loop or hold the wool in their fingers, so that eventually everyone has the wool tied to both hands and it is criss-crossed across the circle.

Ask everyone to look at the structure they have made, ask for comments.

The leader responds.

(AIM: to recognise how each person is a necessary part of the whole.)

The leader then invites:

a   people to raise one hand and lower the other—notice the change in structure;

b   every second person to kneel—again notice the change;

c   every second person to release their hands—what happens?

d   everyone to release their hands—what happens?

While everyone is standing in the circle with the wool structure, the leader reads:

Just as each of our bodies has several parts and each part has a separate function, so all of us, in union with Christ, form one body—and as parts of it we belong to each other. Our gifts differ according to the grace given us.

Romans 12:4–6a

Invite everyone to relax and sit on the floor.
The leader asks:
What does this reading say about what we have just done?

Looking back on the home activity

• Invite the students to share their story of a Christian hero. Discuss the stories of the people who feature in the books and posters displayed.

Agreement

• Have Agreement displayed.
  —How has the Agreement worked?
  —Are there any suggestions for future changes?

Main activity

*W*e belong to the Catholic Christian Community. Baptism is the sign of this belonging. Students display the baptismal stole they have made.
The leader asks the parents:
Using the 'Baptism souvenirs' you have brought, tell your children the story of their Baptism: who came, the date, which church, where, why, how your name was chosen, who were your Godparents.
(The leader may add or delete questions as considered appropriate.)

Conclusion

*T*he leader invites everyone to form a circle, sitting on the floor. In the centre of the circle, have:
- lit candle
- bowl of water
- cottonwool ball, soaked in oil (in a dish)
- loaf of bread or Lebanese bread
- wine glass of grape juice.

The leader asks everyone to open to p. 51 of Student's Book.

Select four students as readers to read the parts of Scripture, after each symbol is introduced.

Close with: prayer for parents (together)
prayer for family (together) p. 52.

Supper

Preparation for the Sacrament

Preparation

- letter writing materials
- paper
- envelopes
- pens
- model letters for display

Welcome activity

Direct each family to read quietly together 'The Sacrament of Confirmation', pp. 54–56, Student's Book.

Agreement

Make sure everyone knows when and where Confirmation will be celebrated.
- What to wear?
- What to do afterwards, will we have a group celebration?

Main activity

a   Student's Book, p. 54, 'The Sacrament of Confirmation'. Explain that it takes place during Mass, after the Gospel.
- Go through the ceremony with the leader being Bishop.
- Take turns then of parents being Bishop, children being Bishop.

b   Give each person paper and envelopes. Explain, using model sheet, that parents write a letter to their child saying what their hopes are for their child. Children write a letter to their parents for what they have done to prepare them for this day.

c   Have both children and parents seal their letters to give to each other on Confirmation Sunday.

Dear . . . .

We hope that . . . .

. . . .

. . . .

love from . . . .

Dear Mum and Dad

Thank you for . . . .

. . . .

love from . . . .

Conclusion

*I*n a circle, letters in envelopes in the centre, a lit candle . . . pray together the prayer 'All powerful God' (Student's Book, p. 55).

Supper